# *Greetings from* THE LANCASHIRE COAST

A NOSTALGIC TRIP UP THE LANCASHIRE COAST

IN PICTURE POSTCARDS

**Catherine Rothwell**
**and**
**Cliff Hayes**

PRINTWISE PUBLICATIONS LIMITED

1992

© Printwise Publications 1992

Published by Printwise Publications Ltd
47 Bradshaw Road, Tottington, Bury, Lancs, BL8 3PW.

Warehouse and Orders
40-42 Willan Industrial Estate, Vere Street,
(off Eccles New Road),
Salford, M5 2GR.
Tel: 061-745 9168 Fax: 061-737 1755

ISBN No. 1 872226 41 8

Series Editor
Cliff Hayes

Printed and bound by Manchester Free Press, Paragon Mill, Jersey Street,
Manchester M4 6FP. Tel 061-236 8822.

# *ACKNOWLEDGEMENTS*

Thanks for help go to Lancashire Library, Blackpool Library, Stanley
Butterworth and Dougie Forton from Culceth, Warrington.

# FOREWORD

In assembling these postcards for 'Greetings from the Lancashire Coast' warm thanks are due to my husband for his help and patience; to Rod Armitage of Crookes Books, Sheffield; to the Red Rose Postcard Club and to Eric Mills of Hyde, Cheshire, for his generous loan of many vintage postcards in mint condition.

That institution, the good old British picture postcard, has been around since 1890 and after stamp collecting may now well be the most popular item. Interest is reflected in the prices commanded by rare and unusual subjects in good condition. Silk postcards from World War 1 can be worth £40; postcards of Edwardian glamour girls painted by famous artists have been sold for £100. Name virtually any subject: Steam; Children's Comics Characters; Disasters; Landscapes; Theatres; Personalities. Somewhere out there you will find postcards about them all.

Understandably, the greatest volume have been and still are devoted to holiday themes. Of all the thousands of happy-go-lucky cards one would expect Blackpool to be in the forefront.

From Blackpool, once described as 'The People's Magnet', greetings cards of every description emanated, but it is interesting to look into the postcard photographer/publishers of other Lancashire towns: Crosland (Arnside); James Atkinson (Ulverston); G. Howarth (Lancaster); Valentines (Blackburn); Sankey (Barrow), W. and N.S. Howarth (St. Anne's); Corona Publishing Company (Blackpool). I cite but a few of those appearing in this book.

Frank Burton, who set up at 70 King William Street, Blackburn, specialised in advertising cards like the Fresh Fleetwood Fish example. He claimed: 'If you own a photograph or print that you would like reproducing on a postcard, you may entrust it to my representative, 24 real photographic postcards for 2/6d.' Artistes performing at the local theatres came to him, even the escapologist Harry Houdini. Of course they did likewise in other towns: Morecambe; Blackpool; Liverpool etc.

At Christmas and New Year delightful private greetings cards were printed. Some are like works of art, expressing a gentler age. The now greatly-prized postcards of A.R. Quinton were reproduced from his paintings. He spent the three months of summer cycling up and down Britain, sketching or painting in oils or water colours; Garstang was one place where he stayed. That was his summer occupation; winter was spent in his studio. His paintings were seen for the first time on postcards in 1910, produced by Raphael Tuck.

*Catherine Rothwell*

# Morecambe — 1950 with plenty to do and see

# ABOUT THE AUTHORS

With his enthusiasm for history and local knowledge Cliff Hayes has again collaborated with experienced Local History author Catherine Rothwell to produce a book that we hope readers will find interesting and informative.

## Catherine Rothwell

Catherine was born in the Prestwich area of Manchester and has resided on the Fylde Coast of Lancashire for the past thirty years. During her career she has been Deputy Borough Librarian of Fleetwood and after re-organisation, in charge of all Local History and Reference for the Lancashire District of Wyre.

Catherine's articles frequently appear in such quality magazines as 'Lancashire Life', 'The Lady', 'Lake Scene'.

Her success in writing has led to appearances on B.B.C. and Granada Television, and Catherine has been interviewed on B.B.C. Radio Lancashire, Radio Piccadilly, Coventry and Warwick, Isle of Man Radio and Red Rose Radio. She enjoys lecturing to the W.E.A. and to local Associations and Groups.

*Catherine Rothwell*

*Cliff Hayes*

## Cliff Hayes

Born 1945 and brought up in The Ball O'Ditton, Widnes (when it was proper and part of Lancashire).

Cliff has been involved in printing since the age of 13. His career has taken him from an apprenticeship in Widnes, via a position as ship's printer with the Shaw-Saville line on round the world cruises, to posts with national newspapers, publishers and printing companies.

He has been settled in Manchester for 20 years, and is happily married with a teenage daughter.

As a publisher he had to get involved and has co-written ten books and has written three books himself.

He can be heard quite regularly on G.M.R. in Manchester as well as Radio Merseyside and Radio Lancashire (where he has had a short series).

Helter Skelter, Water Chute and Flying Machine, Southport.

Before real flying in aeroplanes was readily available, people made do with Stansfield's Patent Aerial Flight. Southport's version of the machine, pictured here, was for years very popular. Nearby were the Helter Skelter, one of my favourites, and the Water Chute, which I never had the nerve to try, but my brothers did.

Another view from early 1900 of the Flying Machine and Water Chute discharging into the large boating lake at Southport. By the 1930's the two ornamental lakes were joined and New Bridge built to form a connecting walkway.

In 1835 Peter Hesketh, who built Fleetwood-on-Wyre, formed a company to build a seawall and handsome marine promenade at Southport. At first a penny toll was charged to walk along it, but after a while it ceased to be charged.

Promenade, Southport.

PROMENADE & LAKE SOUTHPORT

The strollers on the promenade in this 1910 card would not have been bothered by the penny charge as it had been dropped by then.

This 1920's view shows a very busy promenade and lake.

# SOUTHPORT

'What Southport does it generally does well,' was written in the 1900s. This was certainly true of the fairy lights on Lord Street and the illuminated, graceful bandstand where on warm evenings visitors could sit, listening to music, so lengthening their day's pleasure. This Artist's postcard of 1912 showing the Municipal Gardens and Bandstand, depicts all the resort's once-famed elegance, with fountains playing and well dressed crowds promenading.

Botanic Gardens, Southport

The Botanic Gardens are the subject of a 1917 greetings card on which Millie writes to her friend Diana, 'You know, this is a pretty place.' Coming from a mill town, all this cool water, luxuriant trees and tranquility must have been of great benefit. The Cotton Employers and Textile Factor Workers Association had persuaded employers to fix holidays at $136\frac{1}{2}$ hours per annum by 1914. Based on a ten-hour working day, this would amount to $13\frac{1}{2}$ days.

# SOUTHPORT

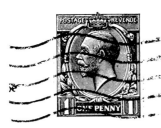

LORD STREET, SOUTHPORT.    Courtesy L.M.S.R.

LORD STREET, SOUTHPORT.    H.9205

Two views of Lord Street in 1931. This street was so popular that other Lancashire Towns copied its name. Laid out on one side with gardens, on the other with shops and cafes, the monumental Cenotaph and Colonnade shown here further added to its concept, along with theatres and hotels.

MARINE DRIVE AND SHORE, SOUTHPORT

A postcard of Marine Drive and Shore in 1932. Southport brought back the receding ocean by means of a very long pier. Since 1863 there had been a pier train running out almost a mile. The train, with its five coaches, can be seen crossing above the crowded beach, which also gives some idea of Southport's popularity at that time.

Yes the sea did come in at Southport; though this card goes right back to 1906 to prove it. Interesting are the two high tide pools for paddling.

# *SOUTHPORT*

High Tide, Southport

An early 1930's card of the high tide. Even at that date this must have been unusual.

ONE PENNY

POST CARD

THE ADDRESS TO BE WRITTEN ON THIS SIDE.

"Land of the
Little People"

TOWN CENTRE, LAND OF THE LITTLE PEOPLE, SOUTHPORT.

VILLAGE OF MERRIVALE, LAND OF THE LITTLE PEOPLE, SOUTHPORT.

The Model Village; one of
the resorts attractions has
been captured in these two
charming cards from
E.T.W. Dennis & Sons Ltd.
'Land of The Little People'
it was called and was a
very popular place to visit
up to the 1970's. These
views are from just after
World War II.

# SOUTHPORT

The names Hesketh and Southport are firmly entwined. Hesketh Park shown here in these two 1930's cards is a beautifully landscaped park kept in pristine condition.

HESKETH PARK, SOUTHPORT

ROSE GARDEN, HESKETH PARK, SOUTHPORT. 22

A tariff card from Stevenson's Private Hotel in Southport, 6/6d for Bed & Breakfast sounds a good deal to me!

Stevenson's Private Hotel

"COURT ROYAL"
13 ALEXANDRA ROAD, SOUTHPORT

Phone 2645                    Mrs. STEVENSON, Proprietress

# TARIFF

THE Hotel has a southern aspect, is close to the Promenade, Lord Street, all Amusements, and within a few minutes of two of the leading Golf Links.

Hot and Cold Water and Gas Fires in Bedrooms.

Separate Tables.   Lounge.

Tennis Court.

Garage arrangements.

Board Residence 9/6 per da
£3 3 0 per week
Special Terms for Children
Tea, Bed and Breakfast, 7/6
"    "    "    *6/6*

**MEAL HOURS :**

BREAKFAST    -    -    -    9 a.m.

DINNERS (Mid-day)    -    -    1 p.m.

HIGH TEA    -    -    -    5 p.m.

LIGHT SUPPER ON RETIRING

# LYTHAM ST. ANNE'S

THE PROMENADE LYTHAM

The promenade at Lytham in about 1900, shows one of the wind shields which were spaced at intervals for the comfort of visitors. Nearby is much digging of holes and building of sand castles. This card was printed around 1902 but posted in 1908.

SOUTH PROMENADE, ST ANNES.

A crisp and neat card from 1912 showing the South Promenade at St. Annes. The Straw Boater hats, the bicycles and horse-drawn carriages show a very genteel St. Annes.

This old postcard of St. Anne's sandhills about 1900 reveals how sand was shifted by a donkey engine. In October 1927, for the first time in its history the tide broke through the sandhills in North Drive St. Anne's and flooded the road to a depth of six feet. Two sunken gardens were flooded and masses of sea weed clung to the buildings. By Ormerod Home the road was under sixteen feet of water resembling a huge lake. Six carts were needed to shift the sand and sea weed from the North Drive.

# LYTHAM ST. ANNE'S

DONKEYS ON THE SANDS. ST ANNES ON THE SEA.

Donkeys on the sands at St. Anne's, backed by a long pier, has to be a long time ago, probably 1905. A horse-drawn ice cream cart from number 82 Garton Street is another nostalgic anachronism. The St. Anne's Pier, opening by Lord Stanley and enlarged several times, was then a great success, attracting promenading crowds. In its early days a German band played in the open-air bandstand during the season. Mr. W.H. Nutter acted as manager and director of the Pier's affairs. Before the change in the channel, a line of fishing boats and innumerable pleasure craft were anchored on each side of the jetty and around the pier were steamboats ready to take parties to Lytham, Southport, Liverpool, Fleetwood or Morecambe.

The most notable day in the history of St. Anne's was the granting of the Charter of Incorporation by which the town advanced from Urban District to the newly constituted Municipal Borough of Lytham St. Anne's on May 1st, 1922. This is another in the series of postcards issued to mark an event for which elaborate arrangements were made, including a luncheon at the Grand Hotel. Church bells rang and lifeboat rockets were fired. Unfortunately, as can be seen, the weather was bad, the whole proceedings taking place in a heavy downpour. The amazing thing was that so many people braved the weather. This view during the Charter Day Celebrations in front of J.R. Taylor's and Mac Fisheries Ltd. is an umbrella manufacturers' delight! The London City and Midland Bank and Shields are also in the picture.

# LYTHAM ST. ANNE'S

The St. Anne's War Memorial Hospital was formally opened on Charter Day by the Earl of Derby (centre) pictured outside the mansion, "Banastre Holme" purchased by the Trustees of the Hospital for £10,000.

Presenting the Charter, May Day 1922. Mr. W. Wolstenholme's photographs of an historic occasion, the presenting of the Charter at the Marton, Blackpool, St. Anne's boundary, was just one of a number of commemorative postcards. Civic dignitaries present were Mr. H.A. Pickup; Mr. P.H. Stephenson; Mr. Albert E. Smith; Councillor T. H. Wood; Councillor Critchley; Mr. T. Bradley; Mr. G Lawson; Councillor W. Dodd; Mr. H.J. Carmont. The Charter Mayor, Mr. J. Talbot Clifton, Lord of the Manor and his son and heir Harry de Vere Clifton were also present.

*Hotel Majestic*, this postcard from about 1926 of the Hotel Majestic at St. Anne's-on-Sea, shows off a fine building, now demolished. The Majestic Celebrity Orchestra conducted by Gerald Bright (below) used to play here in 1926, broadcasting three times a week in those early days of radio. Gerald Bright was later known as the dance band leader Geraldo. Upon this site is now built a block of luxury flats.

# LYTHAM ST. ANNE'S

THE LAKE, ASHTON GARDENS, ST ANNES.

A local card from Leach's Visitor Series, St. Anne's, posted in the early years of World War I. The card tells Mrs. L. Taylor back in Otley Road, Leeds that F.L. North is recovering and getting stronger - maybe a soldier on convalescence?

The well laid out gardens on the promenade in the mid 1920s.

STEPPING STONES, PROMENADE.

BRIDGE, PROMENADE GARDENS

WATERFALL, PROMENADE.

BOATING POOL.

PROMENADE AND PIER.

ST ANNES · ON · SEA

BOATING POOL.

SQUARE AND CRESCENT.

ROSE GARDEN, ASHTON GARDENS.

G 4427

This composite card from 1949 by Valentine's, shows how pleasant St. Anne's was with 'civic pride' bursting at the seams.

POST CARD

THE ADDRESS TO BE WRITTEN ON THIS SIDE.

# LYTHAM ST. ANNE'S

The crowds in this 1930's postcard are enjoying themselves on beautiful, golden sand on the North Beach, St. Anne's, which, alas are no more as spartina grass and pollution from the River Ribble have taken their toll. This sight would have delighted the St. Anne's Land and Building Company Ltd., led by Elijah Hargreaves, registered October 4th 1874. They set out to build 'the opal of the west' and the town's rise from sandhills was phenomenal, but after the promenade and public gardens were built a depression set in. This was relieved by the building of the pier in 1886 and again buildings rapidly multiplied.

*Post Card*

Issued at the same time as the previous card was this fine example showing the splendour of St. Anne's Bathing Pool.

St. Anne's Boating Pool pictured in 1925 on the reverse of which is printed 'Greetings from St. Anne's-on-Sea.'

## LYTHAM ST. ANNE'S

THE PROMENADE, ST. ANNES-ON-SEA.

Views of the Boating Pool, Gardens, Shelters, Pier and wide promenade feature in this sharp picture postcard of the promenade in the early 1940's. Visitors are relaxing in corporation deck chairs, and babies asleep in perambulators. Five young ladies out for a stroll at St. Anne's-on-Sea.

A dramatic postcard of a ship named the 'Huntcliff' which was stranded on the beach at St. Anne's in 1894. Local photographers were not slow, and many postcards were sold that summer showing the ship before she was refloated undamaged.

The Grotto, part of the sheltered gardens laid out in the early years of the resort. Sea pebbles were cunningly set to create pictures to delight visitors. Nearby Lytham's Bath Street has some particularly good examples.

A greetings card of 1902 Lytham long before its amalgamation with St. Anne's in 1922. The Promenade, Lytham Green, the famous white windmill, the lifeboat houses, 'Charlie's Mast' and ornamental shelters are all present. 'Leafy Lytham' was always a favourite for people who preferred quiet holidays and the green of the countryside. This card is from Florrie in the Cottage Hospital at Lytham to say she is getting better and stronger to her friends in Leeds.

The Promenade, Lytham.

# LYTHAM ST. ANNE'S

St. Anne's Lifeboat Launch 1900s

Issued by the local paper 'The St. Anne's Express', this 2 view nautical card accents the Lifeboat Service. Practice launches always drew a crowd and the real thing was even more exciting. St. Anne's lifeboat crew were lost in 1886 trying to rescue the men from the German barque 'Mexico'.

# BLACKPOOL

Whitegate Drive, Blackpool

CIRCULAR TOUR

PROMENADE

78

A Circular Tour was made by toastrack tram number 78 seen here about 1924 clanging along Whitegate Drive, an area that in the 19th Century was just a country road. Visitors also loved the drive to Cherry Tree Gardens, developed by Mr. and Mrs. Fisher from Cherry Tree Farm and nursery gardens. In 1919 Blackpool Corporation bought the Blackpool to Fleetwood trams and gradually the many livery stables with their hundreds of horses became garages. Published for the Corporation by the Corona Publishing Co in the 20s.

The festoon of lights on this tram is a reminder of the famous Blackpool Illuminations, of which 1992 was the 60th Anniversary. Staged outside Wakes weeks, in September and October, they bring about eight million people who spend £70 million visiting 'the greatest free show on earth'.

## TUCK'S POST CARD

CARTE POSTALE.   ——————   POSTKARTE.

# BLACKPOOL

Blackpool was the first holiday resort in the country to undertake systematic publicity. Since 1879 a rate had been levied annually for this purpose, resulting in press campaigns, thousands of picture postcards, picture posters and official guides and brochures. This brought in the visitors.

This postcard from the summer of 1910 shows what was then known as New Promenade. 'We are having a grand time,' wrote Nell. 'The weather is beautiful. But there are millions here. We saw the flying on Sunday from our street.'

Published by Tuck and the Blackpool Corporation to promote the Circular tour around 1920.

This postcard from early 1900's shows a crowded steamer setting off on another very popular sea trip. Sailings from Central Pier by the Blackpool Passenger Steamboat Co. Ltd. (weather and other circumstances permitting) were made by the fast saloon passenger steamers 'Queen of the North', 'Wellington' and 'Bickerstaffe' (pictured here). Their destinations were Llandudno, Southport, Douglas, Morecambe Bay and Fleetwood Light, and the trips added to the excitement and variation of the holidays. Pity they don't still sail!

These visitors, the Briggs family, were photographed at Eddison Studios, 14 Manchester Terrace, Blackpool.

It was quite the done thing to go on holiday and have your photograph taken, either in a studio as a family, or with a landmark behind you. On your first or second day and certainly by the middle of the week, you were sending home cards of yourself, proving that you were really there.

Throughout the Edwardian period and in the 1920's visitors to Blackpool found wonderful entertainment programmes with the Tower, Winter Gardens, Palace, Grand Theatre and Opera House, plus numerous other halls, open every day of the year. At the Grand Theatre and Opera House Mr. C.J. Abud's Company presented the 'Prisoner of Zenda' on February 13th 1899.

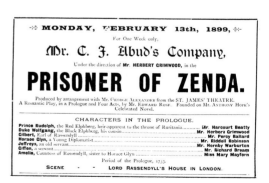

A lovely old greetings postcard from 1903, the days of Kettlewell's, Outfitters, across from the ornamental drinking fountain in Talbot Square, alongside which is a waiting landau. With a delivery van (horse-drawn, of course) and a Dreadnought tram this greetings card has got everything from the early years of the century. William H. Cocker laid the foundation stone for the drinking fountain in 1870. What a pity it had to go!

The 'E.R.G. Victoria Series' went in for the picturesque and here we have another dramatic sunset over North Pier. 'I am enjoying myself a treat,' writes Annie in August 1907 but Jack adds, 'Weather cold and drink rather off.'

# BLACKPOOL

One of my favourite Blackpool cards. Still the gardens on the prom, the trams running in the road and the boats drawn up on the front. This card sent in 1904 but the picture probably dates from 1900.

THE FAIR GROUND, SOUTH SHORE. (No. L.27)

The Corona Publishing Company issued this greetings card of the Fair Ground with the Flying Machine, Scenic Railway and Lighthouse Helter Skelter, the last mentioned being imported from America in 1905. It immediately became a picture postcard subject, so this card is 1906. The straw hats cannot dispel the sombre look of the clothes of holiday makers. I think this was taken on a cool day.

This is a good example of a 'doctored' card. A photograph of the Water Chute just after the turn of the century has had a couple super-imposed on it, and the water splash is scratched on, and the card printed in about 1908. Posted July 1909 from a young man R. Rushton missing his sweetheart back in Pike Laith Farm, Waterside in Colne. In 1911 to celebrate the Coronation of King George V and Queen Mary, children were given the 'freedom' of Blackpool: free tram rides, gala sports, ox-roasting, bonfire, and free rides at South Shore.

Water Chute Blackpool      I am quite "carried away" by the delights of this place

Three in a donkey cart 1911. This fun postcard was taken in the Electric Studios, 12 Bank Hey Street, Blackpool. There are many variations on these comic cards including this one showing a couple in a mock-up of a flying machine from 1910.

A 1920 card shows the splendour and grandeur of the Savoy Hotel and it's well laid out gardens.

This 1910 postcard showing Grahame White flying round Blackpool Tower was sent by a very excited couple who had spent the day watching the flights over the town.

Aviation Week, Fylde Coast, October 18-23, 1909, Blackpool would have had the first Air Pageant in Britain had not Doncaster beaten it by three days. Twenty thousand people turned up for the actual event, to witness the Frenchman M. Rougier remain in the air almost half an hour. Lancashire's own A. V. Roe, tried to fly but travelled only 100 yards, never taking off. He decided his propellers were too large and would have to get fresh ones. The Blackpool Tower Company offered a prize to the first British aviator who piloted an all-British machine and covered 100 yards without touching the ground, but it was the French who covered themselves with glory on this occasion.

# BLACKPOOL

Destroyed by fire in December 1956, the Tower Ballroom was restored at a cost of a quarter of a million pounds. Forty tons of scaffolding were needed for plaster craftsmen, gilders and artists, many brought out of retirement for this skilled reconstruction. A thousand gallons of paint and 6,750 books of gold leaf were used in the worthwhile task of restoration. This wonderful card shows Blackpool Tower Ballroom in all its original magnificence. Posted August 1907, the writer J.H. uses a lovely phrase 'I am enjoying myself up to the fan light' when writing to her friend Eliza Rimmer in Colne.

Indian Lounge, Winter Gardens 1910; another ambitiously ornate setting dreamed up by Blackpool councillors was the Indian Lounge in the Winter Gardens, the dome of which towered to the height of 120 feet and measured 126 feet in circumference. The Winter Gardens were opened in June 1878 by the then Lord Mayor of London, Sir Thomas Owden, with 60 other mayors and mayoresses from all over the country.

'LOVE TO MY FRIEND' from Blackpool; a charming card written in September 1915 includes six facets of Blackpool decked out with roses, crowded scene on the sands, a storm featuring 'the Dog Wave', North Promenade and Princess Parade with the Metropole, which was according to an old Blackpool Times Year Book originally Dickson's Hotel. The hand clasp is a nice touch in this highly collectable greetings card from a 'FLORAL COMPOSITE' series put out around 1910 from Woolston Brothers.

'COME TO BLACKPOOL'. This 1918 postcard. It shows the Gynn Inn, North Shore, with an inset of beautiful actress Gladys Cooper, every girl's ideal at the time. The old Gynn Inn, which was pulled down some years later, is already looking out of place with a 'Dreadnought' tram passing and one motor vehicle. 1918 was the year Prime Minister David Lloyd George was made an Honorary Freeman of Blackpool. He collected the award personally, in Blackpool, four years later.

## *BLACKPOOL*

South Promenade from the Manchester Hotel; in a 1919 postcard with the crowds in evidence and a couple with a bassinette at the top of a slade. In 1916 Promenade extensions were commenced from Victoria Pier to the southern boundary where Blackpool Borough adjoined the Borough of Lytham St. Anne's. Two slades were constructed, one opposite Watson's Road and the other opposite Harrowside.

An early 1900 card showing the Town Hall in Talbot Square.

This commemorative card shows Blackpool Tower and the beach in 1926 when the Big Wheel was also part of the landscape. Central Beach with its horse-drawn bathing vans is shown as being busy and the tower of St. John's Church can be made out between the tower and the wheel. In this particular summer 1,000 Advertising Men ascended the Tower to 'gain the Wide Horizon's grander view'. It was all part of a scheme entitled Advertising Lancashire, an occasion when the publicity men of Great Britain were welcomed to the town.

Of all postcards sent from Blackpool the most desirable was that one stamped 518 feet up, 'from the top of the Tower'. This striking view shows the upper structure with the town visible below, possibly dating from the 1950's and published by Aerofilms of Boreham Wood, Herts.

A classical example of Victorian architecture, The Tower, on October 10th, 1973 was declared a Grade II listed building and has just reopened after a facelift.

41

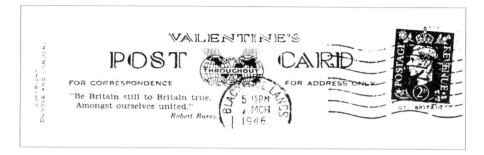

Although posted in March 1946 the card looks to have been printed during the war as most cards were black and white or single colour to meet UTILITY standard. This one was printed in Brown to give it a 'sepia' look and the series was titled 'PHOTO BROWN'. It also has a printed verse to lift the spirits and inspire patriotism.

Five views of Stanley Park on this postcard include the grand fountain, Rose Garden and Boating Lake of 26 acres opened on October 2nd, 1926 along with the new Marine Promenade. In the formal gardens were placed 'statuary of most exceptional merit', which included two lead lions based on the Medici Collection presented by John Magee. The park was designed by Thomas Henry Mawson and Edward Prentice Mawson, Landscape Architects of Lancaster, and the cost of the whole scheme was £250,000.

Blackpool Illuminations are a spectacular treat always worth returning to. Usually the most spectacular displays of the illuminations are the tableaux at Bispham and the Pleasure Beach at South Shore. Here the Pleasure Beach is photographed by night at the end of the 1920's. Every year thousands of visitors are drawn from all over the country to this unique display. The 50th display was in 1982 when new features such as Maritime England appeared at a cost of £870,000.

*Pleasure Beach, S.S., Blackpool, by Night.*

CENTRAL PROMENADE, BLACKPOOL.

A nice crisp card from about 1959 showing Blackpool front just before its 1960 facelift. Though only 33 years ago the cars captured on the card bring back a flood of memories.

# BLACKPOOL

ROCKERY PROMENADE, NORTH SHORE, BLACKPOOL.

Rockery Promenade, North Shore 1936; the square-towered Cabin Lift on the skyline no longer works and the semi-circular boating lake has been altered. High seas in winter carried the boats away on more than one occasion. The Rockery Promenade helped to prevent further erosion of cliffs, which over the years had occurred on a massive scale.

# BISPHAM

The Cliffs Bispham.

An unusual card showing couples relaxing on the cliffs at Bispham about 1909. Although Blackpool's pier is just discernible on the horizon of this picture, there was then little at Bispham beyond the Cliffs and quaint village to which Blackpool visitors walked or rode out to by wagonette, many to have tea at the Tincklers' Ivy Cottage Tea Rooms. The crumbling nature of the cliffs is evident. Cliff falls occurred so these couples were taking a chance.

The Beach, Bispham.

Although this card is from the early 1920s Bispham still had its sand dunes, starr grass, cliffs and pleasant beach without crowds. Some boating had been introduced by local fishermen and shrimpers.

# BISPHAM

The date July 20th 1920 has been written on front and back of this postcard showing the Front at Bispham, the writer declaring it 'a swank place'. Quieter than Blackpool and slower to develop, Bispham is much older. 'Blackpoole' was recorded in 1602 whereas Bispham, an Anglian settlement, was in being in the year 700. A few boarding houses have been built, but, with no benches provided, visitors are sitting on the cliff top road verge. Published locally by T Murgatroyd, a local tradesman in Bispham.

The Front, Bispham.

July 20. 1920

THE VILLAGE, BISPHAM.

In this postcard from the 1930s Bispham still retains the rural air of an old village which had its smithy and wheelwright's shop and was surrounded by farms; in the 1880s there were 20. The old, white-washed cottages on the right, along with the blacksmith's premises, were destined to go by the 1960s. and a bus service has obviously already arrived. Bispham was always a popular outing from Blackpool and motor charabancs began to bring in more and more visitors.

A rare very early photo of Bispham, emphasises just how rural the village was in 1880s. All Hallows Church tower dominates what was referred to then as 'the pretty village near Blackpool.'

All Hallows Church in 1978.

# THORNTON-CLEVELEYS

Sea View is an example of the solid boarding houses that were built along the front at Cleveleys. Mr. Sykes, the local chemist, had a number of such properties photographed and made into greetings cards available about 1906 for sale to visitors.

Victoria Road, Cleveleys in August 1908 is worlds away from today's traffic-laden highway. This Valentine's card has children playing in what was anciently known as Ramper Road. On the left is the Cleveleys Hotel. The writer of this card was so fascinated by the high tide that she felt she could have sat and watched it all night.

Promenade, Cleveleys.

A 1927 view of Cleveleys Promenade with Punch and Judy booth, donkeys, boating and the wooden refreshment hut on the beach where the renowned Cleveleys Gingerbreads were sold. After the Jubilee Gardens improvements this safe bathing area acquired a portable water slide and raft. The 1920s and 30s were also the great days of Cleveleys Hydro with its 18 hole golf course, resident orchestra and hydropathic baths. At this time there were still many thatched cottages with quaint names such as; Woodbine, Willow, Oulder Nook etc.

The New Promenade included the Arena which features in this greetings card from the 1930s Progress series. Billed as the 'premier open-air theatre of the North', the Arena offered three performances daily, 11 a.m., 3 p.m. and 7 p.m. from Whit Saturday throughout the season. Charlie and the Follies were appearing about the time of this card.

THE ARENA, PROMENADE, CLEVELEYS.

208629

## FLEETWOOD

Greetings from Fleetwood 1909; The Mount and Mount Gardens are shown in this delightful old picture postcard, which can truly be called a greetings card. These cards were produced with different views inside and indeed these 2 ladies can be found Greeting you from Blackpool and Morecambe as well.

Besides sending off kippers from the Kipper Shop and greetings cards to their friends, visitors to Fleetwood also liked to see the fish landed. This 1920s card shows 'Thrush', a fishing boat, in dock. Deck hands and 'lumpers' are very busy. Loaded coal wagons and cranes can be seen the background. From this fish dock trains ran straight to Billingsgate, London, and other parts of the country.

A very clever card produced in Saxony about 1910 with the Postman's satchel not only bearing the greetings but it opens and contains 10 small views of the town. It was a very popular card and again produced in similar style for most of the growing resorts.

P.S. "LADY EVELYN" BARROW AND FLEETWOOD SERVICE.

Paddle steamer 'Lady Evelyn', shown in this greetings card from the early years of the century, was sailing every weekday in the season between Fleetwood and Barrow. Leaving Fleetwood at 10.15 a.m., this boat arrived at Ramsden Dock at 11.45. The return fare was three shillings, but only two shillings if you travelled 'fare-cabin'. Between May 1st. and September 30th. Tourists' Weekly Tickets were available for an unlimited number of journeys over a period of seven days. Many were the greetings cards sent by tourists. 'Lady Evelyn', renamed 'Brighton Belle', ended her days at the evacuation from Dunkirk in 1940.

The famous four-master 'Lawhill', built in 1892 for C.
Barrie of Dundee, visited Fleetwood when cargo trade
was very busy at the port. Her most famous ship's
master was Gustaf Erikson, who also captained
'L'Avenir'. Visitors were allowed to inspect the
scrubbed, snow-white decks, gleaming brasswork and
neatly stowed sails whilst she lay moored in dock.
Such ships made good photographs for greetings
cards, as this 1900 card shows.

POST    CARD

The old postcard of Wyre Dock, Fleetwood, showing
many masted sailing ships is another example.

ON BOARD THE LADY MOYRA

FLEETWOOD TO BARROW FOR THE LAKES, SEPT. 8/13    2    SANKEY, PHOTO PRESS, BARROW.

Passengers on board 'Lady Moyra', another of the Barrow boats, on September 8th. 1913. Photographed on the outward journey, they could collect their picture postcards on the way back in the evening, complete with the name of the boat and the date on the bottom.

Steam Ship Woolwich is seen stranded on the Tiger's Tail in September 1909. Strandings and wreckings were all newsworthy subjects on greetings postcards to be sent home by interested visitors. They usually appeared within hours of being taken.

"S.S. WOOLWICH", AGROUND AT FLEETWOOD, SEPT. 1909

Twenty years ago Fleetwood visitors were sending cards like this Lillywhite combination from the 1970s.

POST CARD
THE ADDRESS TO BE WRITTEN
ON THIS SIDE.

# FLEETWOOD

"DUKE OF CONNAUGHT"
FLEETWOOD & BELFAST SERVICE

Duke of Connaught 1915

Featured in this postcard of the London North Western
Railway Series, April 1905, is the 'Duke of Connaught', one of
the steamers that sailed regularly on the Fleetwood-Belfast
route.

A sedate group of beautifully dressed young ladies from the Parish Church of St. Peter, Fleetwood, who appeared in a concert on Fleetwood Pier June 19, 1911. Front seats cost one shilling and they were tip-up and plush.

Fleetwood Fresh Fish Supply Company 1919

The Fleetwood Fresh Fish Supply Company issued this combined cheery postcard and price list. The sou'westered old salt and molly hamper full of prime fish go back to 1919 when prices were amazing: whole cod, conger, bream, gurnet 6 lbs. for 2 shillings, 30lb, for 7 shillings; class 2 soles, turbot, brill, salmon, mackerel, live lobster, 'in packages at 2 shillings, 3 shillings, 5 shillings'. The slogan was, 'Fish best bought is fish fresh caught.' Those were the days of record catches.

# *FLEETWOOD*

A turn of the century photo showing the Knott End-Fleetwood Ferry leaving for Knott End and over dressed children playing on the beach.

Established 1912

# SILVER GREY
## LUXURY COACHES

### DAILY TOURS TO LAKELAND
AND ALL PLACES OF INTEREST

Large Fleet of Observation Coaches to seat 500 persons

### SEVEN DAY DE-LUXE HOLIDAY TOURS
TO ALL PARTS OF GREAT BRITAIN WITH
ACCOMMODATION AT FIRST - CLASS HOTELS

### Private Parties our Speciality

All Enquiries, large or small, receive prompt attention

No Holiday is Complete without a "Silver Grey" Tour

MORECAMBE MOTORS LTD Harbour Garage Morecambe.

These two views of Lancaster Road, Knott End, are both from 1908 and show the unchanged, rural nature of Over-Wyre which visitors so much appreciated. Whitewashed cottages, small tea shops, the only 'traffic' a bicycle, old-fashioned telegraph poles and ankle-length, sweeping skirts are all signs of long ago. So is standing in the middle of the road.

# KNOTT END

When Knott End decided to become a resort the name St. Bernard's-on-Sea was tried but it would not stick. This 1928 montage shows the Ferry Slade, Dolly's Cottage (now gone), the Esplanade, Wyre light (now disused) and the Hackensall Woods. 'Having a lovely time here, weather glorious,' writes Nellie.

The arrival of Ferry Boat "Bourne" May c. 1920 at the foot of Knott End's slade. A trip on the ferry to Knott End was a must for Blackpool visitors with a sense of adventure after the tram journey all the way to Fleetwood. Across the River Wyre the outline of Fleetwood shows from the right, lifeboat house, Lower Lighthouse, North Euston Hotel and on the left tall Pharos Lighthouse.

A postcard of the Bourne Arms Hotel about the same year shows its restaurant where steaks were a speciality, as was the ice cream. Crowds came from Fleetwood to sample it.

The Shore, Knott End. This 1930s picture postcard has houseboats decked out with bunting as subject. On the beach at Knott End in the 30s were five of these old craft hired as holiday homes in season. Beyond are old fishermen's cottages, Sea Dyke.

Three likely lads, possibly members of the Territorials or naval reserves, have come to Camp at Lancaster, 15 Oct 1932. There was always a photographer on hand as the lads liked to send postcards home to their families.

Market Street, Lancaster about 1900

The London and North Western Railway's Parcel Office is on the right. An empty coal cart is approaching the Storey Institute where the Public Library was and Castle Station could also be reached up the rise. Published locally by Millington the Stationers in Lancaster.

Greetings from Kent's Bank House, an advertising card. Sent by guests at the house enjoying what seems to be a spacious and well-ordered hotel. Pictures seem to be from around 1912.

The Sands. Morecambe.

Brett's Publications, 'My Pocket Novels', 'Something to Read' and 'Keepsake Novels', supplied a series of Fine Art Post cards free with their books, of which this, The Sands, Morecambe Bay, is one. It is a splendid scene from the 1900s with the usual beach activity: paddling, pleasure boat trips, oyster stall, straw hats and the inevitable black umbrella fending off the sun. Most of these cards are unfranked when you come across them, or have been just used up as reminder postcards.

MORECAMBE.

A very early card showing a sedate Morecambe about 1900.

# MORECAMBE

The Bay, Morecambe.

This 1905 postcard shows early summer crowds, a quaint horse-drawn tram, yachts in Morecambe Bay and the pier decked in flags. A good view could be enjoyed from the pier roof garden.

In October 1927 when floods surged the length of the Lancashire coast Morecambe's West End Pier broke in two and a portion was blown away in the hurricane. Huge holes were torn in the promenade and dancers marooned in a hall where the floods burst into the boiler house and put the place in darkness. In Lancashire 12 people were killed in those few days.

Recently it has been very sad to watch the pier being cut up and finally dismantled. To see the fine craftsmanship and elegant ironwork just cut to pieces seems to lack finer feelings, and reflects the ruthless commercialism of management today.

THE SANDS, WEST END MORECAMBE N°C 144

The Sands, West End Morecambe in 1907. Notice the small folding chairs rather than deck chairs which were to be so popular later on. Most visitors seem to prefer to paddle or stroll about.

# MORECAMBE

This card from 1907 features the Clock Tower recently presented to the town by John Robert Birkett who was Mayor from 1903 to 1906.

THE CLOCK TOWER, MORECAMBE.

It is also featured in this card from a few years later, with a wagonette at the kerb waiting for customers, the same old pillar box, lots of graceful sailing boats and a lovely ornate street lamp which would now be a collector's item.

Watching the swimmers was a very popular spectator sport in 1937 when this card was sent. An interesting photo of the busy swimming baths.

W.M. Doyle, the Crescent, Morecambe, published this card of West End Promenade in 1911. The Promenade is still without motorised traffic but is well built up. In the background can be seen the graceful Bandstand. The Promenade stretched from the west of the Borough to Bare at the east, laid out with rock gardens and walks.

# MORECAMBE

A 1937 combination card showing the pride of the town. Morecambe was indeed proud of its attractions and believed in the town motto "Beauty surrounds, Health abounds".

Morecambe Bay at sundown was one of the most sought-after greetings cards. this one dating from 1909. "I am sending you a sunset because you are so fond of them," writes Maria to Lizzie. She was staying at 16 Marine Road. Sunsets were long-famed. "The sun goes down splendidly beyond the Irish Sea, all Lakeland catches the glow," wrote one visitor.

Another Sunset View this one from 1905 and a local production from Morrel and Sons, 17 Alexandra Road, Morecambe.

# *MORECAMBE*

Bare Village, Morecambe. A pleasant study of the village centre taken very early this century. I'm still trying to work out if that gent was really there or pasted on.

A late 1950s combination card shows the best of Bare. I like the model railway and its full coaches.

This lovely postcard, a New Era Series published and printed in Morecambe, shows West End Pier and Bandstand in September 1911. In the foreground is a horse-drawn wagonette waiting for visitors to fill it up. Long black skirts, white blouses, picture hats and umbrellas are in evidence on a sunny day. Without an umbrella one took refuge in the ornamental shelter on the Promenade, which appears to be full.

'We ought to be staying four weeks instead of four days,' writes Fred staying at 7 Victoria Street, Morecambe in August 1911. A beautiful card, of packed sands. Hope you can pick out the steam boats and the Furness fells in the background. In the foreground, rowing boats, paddlers, enormous crowds and well posed centrally, a white umbrella, perhaps starting a new fashion.

# MORECAMBE

Eidsforth Terrace and Tower, Morecambe.

This postcard showing crowds at Eidsforth Terrace and tower when the tide is fully in dates from the end of the first World War. Sea bathing at Morecambe was popular as far back as 1820 when the population was only 400 and Morecambe was known as Poulton. People came out from Lancaster in a coach called 'The Old Times'. Most of this crowd would be back on the beach swimming or paddling when the tide went out. The Tower, once one of the town's main attractions, was built in the Eastern style of architecture with domes and minarets.

STORM AT MORECAMBE                    RELIABLE SERIES. 655 / 36

Storm scenes and crashing waves always sold very well. 'We have got very comfortable lodgings,' writes Cissie, and with such rough weather they would need them. On Sunday September 21st. 1924 Morecambe experienced the fury of an 85 m.p.h. gale which did considerable damage, whipping the sea to frenzy, and on February 27th. 1903 there was another great storm with wind velocity of 87 m.p.h. Storms made the tide at its height several feet deeper and if high tide coincides with the highest velocity of the wind, seas pour over the promenade and down adjacent streets.

'Off for a ride, Morecambe,' reads this postcard which, like so many from there, refers on reverse to a trip to the nearby Lake District posted 1923 but printed much earlier. A very young and not too pleased donkey boy is in attendance.

The Central Beach and Pier about 1930. This card has an innocence from a past age. The long jetty next to the pier is noteworthy. Morecambe fishermen had to keep their eyes on the tide as there was no harbour and boats had to be back at their moorings before the full ebb. The 'nobbies', which collected shrimps, oysters etc., were moored near Central Pier.

# MORECAMBE

The Midland Hotel Morecambe 1933. This fine building style of the 1930s, erected at a time when Morecambe was busy and prosperous, has been used for a Hercule Poirot film in the television series.

Midland Hotel Morecambe.

WINTER GARDENS, MORECAMBE.

*The Winter Gardens, 1969.* This stretch of Morecambe's West End Promenade housed many fine buildings, one of the most prominent being the Winter Gardens owned by theatre managers W.H. Broadhead and Son who provided various kinds of amusements. In the Empress Hall, dancing and skating could be enjoyed whilst billiards and bowls were also available.

Bamforth's 1960s greetings card from Morecambe included the new venture, Sandylands.

The sailing ship 'Moby Dick' was moored at Morecambe when this card was posted but unfortunately was destroyed by fire in June 1970, 'Moby Dick' was originally launched at Glasson Dock in 1887, as 'Ryelands'. This three masted schooner had been used as setting for a number of films and was a good tourist attraction.

# MORECAMBE

Although not a serious rival to those of Blackpool, Morecambe Illuminations in 1962 at Happy Mount Park were acknowledged to be very pretty and helped to extend the season.

This 1968 Bamforth greetings postcard 'I've forgotten all about WORK at Morecambe' features stretches of gardens and promenade, but the difference now is the traffic. Private cars and a motor bus sweep past the Clock Tower, one of Morecambe's landmarks.

# *HEYSHAM*

Main St, Heysham.

This is the main street, Heysham, early this century with Mrs. Kellet's well known tea rooms on the right. The ancient village of Heysham is supposed to have got its name from the 'ham' or dwelling place of Hesse, a warlike Anglian chief. To this day the old-world atmosphere attracts visitors by its tea shops and cottages selling nettle beer brewed locally. These cottages are centuries old.

# *HEYSHAM*

The Village Pump at Heysham.

The Village Pump at Heysham makes a beautiful rural scene and the two views indicate the change between 1900 and 1913. The Novelty Postcard Company issued the earlier one of the old lady and the three boys. Notice the old farm cart in the background with big wheels and tilted shafts.

The later card by the fine company Valetines shows the addition of extra buildings.

Village Pump, Heysham

THE OLD CHURCH. HEYSHAM. 43.

This greetings card of St. Peter's Church was sent in 1939. The Church has traces of 10th. century masonry; the chancel is Norman for it was a Norman rector who made new this Saxon Church. A saxon doorway and hog-back tombstone carved with quaint animals and figures, the shaft of a 9th. century cross proclaim the great age of this foundation. The wonderful view from the church causes many to send it home as a card.

POST CARD

# *HEYSHAM*

Morecambe Bay Holiday Camp, Heysham

This card of the Tower at Morecambe Bay Holiday Camp, at Heysham hides the fun and enjoyment that the camp gave to millions.

NEW PROMENADE & SUNNY SLOPES, HEYSHAM.

A wartime postcard shows visitors and holidaymakers content to sit and stroll on the New promenade and slopes in 1940. Colour cards were not printed during W.W.2 under the austerity rules so companies printed in brown and called the cards 'Sepia' Series; 'Photo Brown'; 'Silver' Series; and other twee names.

# *GRANGE-OVER-SANDS*

This early postcard of Grange-over-Sands in the late 19th. century refers to the town as 'this tiny Torquay of Lancashire.... Only at certain hours is the jetty accessible to steamers that come across from Morecambe.' The jetty can be seen in the distance amongst this general view from the Gardens which were laid out in the 1880s and which flourished in the mild climate and shelter provided by the hills overlooking Leven and Kent estuaries.

Grange-over-Sands, The Pier.

Holiday mood is expressed in this postcard of Grange-over-Sands pier, about 1909, with visitors strolling and watching the shipping. Steamboats came from Morecambe but only when the swift-flowing tide made it possible. However, there were trips out to Holme Island, the local fishermen acting as guides.

# BOLTON-LE-SANDS

Bolton-le-Sands 890

1906; a thick screen of trees protected Bolton-le-Sands from the sea winds blowing off Morecambe Bay. In the church vestry was a photograph of Allen Bell who sang in the choir for 50 years until 1912. This picture postcard shows the top of the ancient Church Tower on the right (15th. century) and the quiet nature of the village in those early years. One man with horse and cart is the only conveyance disturbing the peace.

# SILVERDALE

St John of God Hospital and Noviciate, Silverdale

Even today Silverdale has a great variety of old cottages, houses and farms, many of limestone, this building being the St. John of God Hospital and Noviciate on a postcard from the early 1920s. The railway line from Lancaster to Ulverston brought the first visitors to Silverdale. Elizabeth Gaskell came regularly with her family and stayed at Gibraltar Tower.

# SILVERDALE

The unspoiltness and remoteness that shows in these 3 1930s cards of Silverdale is still there today. Jenny Brown's point has always been a popular but quiet picnic spot and I've enjoyed quite a few picnics there myself. Worth looking for.

The Shore, Silverdale.

The Cave, Silverdale Shore.

Jenny Brown's Point, Silverdale.

# ARNSIDE

Arnside from North End, 1902. Arnside rivalled Grange-over-Sands as a popular Morecambe Bay holiday resort and many greetings cards were sent from there especially in the early 20th. century. With Grange on one side of the estuary and Arnside on the other, visitors liked to 'do' both and include a ramble on Arnside Knott. Pleasure boats sailed from the stone jetty, which was destroyed by floods in 1977 but has since been made good.

ARNSIDE BAY & VIADUCT

A very wide view of the viaduct and bay at Arnside. Crossing this viaduct by train has always been quite a thrill. Another wartime card this one named 'Gravo' Style.

# BARROW-IN-FURNESS

Barrow-in-Furness Town hall, 1908. On clear days Barrow-in-Furness Town Hall Clock was visible through telescope from the Mount Pavilion, Fleetwood and people vied with each other to tell the time by it. Barrow was once a seaside resort until its shipbuilding and other industries became more important.

Furness Abbey, East View, early 1900s. This is a card issued by the Furness Railway to persuade visitors to travel on their line to see the magnificent ruins near Barrow-in-Furness. Instructions to Furness Abbey Station were on the reverse. The Furness Abbey Hotel was beautifully situated within the Abbey Grounds.

FURNESS ABBEY, EAST VIEW.

The English lakeland posters issued by the Railway Company described the district as 'always beautiful in sunlight or moonlight.'

Furness Railway, 1941.

The Furness Railway brought visitors to the coast and the Lake District. The locomotives made interesting postcards. This card shows engine number 89, built in 1875, also the tender of engine number 71.

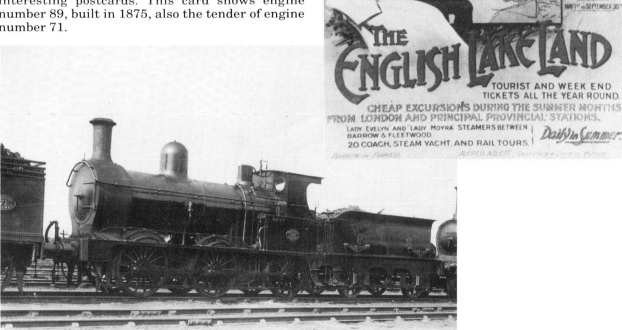

# OTHER BOOKS IN THIS SERIES

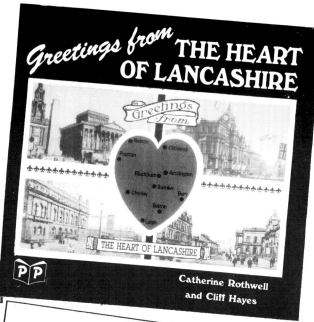

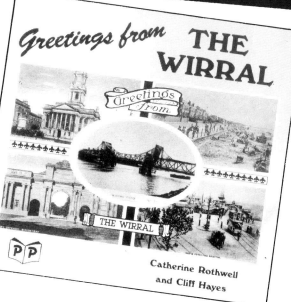

# NORTHERN CLASSIC REPRINTS

## The Manchester Man
### (Mrs. G. Linnaeus Banks)

Re-printed from an 1896 illustrated edition — undoubtedly the finest limp-bound edition ever. Fascinating reading, includes Peterloo. Over 400 pages, wonderfully illustrated.

ISBN 1 872226 16 7 £4.95

## The Manchester Rebels
### (W Harrison Ainsworth)

A heady mixture of fact and fiction combined in a compelling story of the Jacobean fight for the throne of England. Manchester's involvement and the formation of the Manchester Regiment. Authentic illustrations.

ISBN 1 872226 29 9 £4.95

## Hobson's Choice (the Novel)
### (Harold Brighouse)

The humorous and classic moving story of Salford's favourite tale. Well worth re-discovering this enjoyable story. Illustrated edition. Not been available since 1917, never before in paperback.

ISBN 1 872226 36 1 £4.95

# NORTHERN CLASSIC REPRINTS

## Poems & Songs Of Lancashire
### (Edwin Waugh)

A wonderful quality reprint of a classic book by undoubtedly one of Lancashire's finest poets. First published 1859 faithfully reproduced. Easy and pleasant reading, a piece of history.

ISBN 1 872226 27 2 £4.95

## The Dock Road
### (J. Francis Hall RN)

A seafaring tale of old Liverpool. Set in the 1860s, with the American Civil War raging and the cotton famine gripping Lancashire. Period illustrations.

ISBN 1 872226 37 X £4.95

## The Lancashire Witches
### (W. Harrison Ainsworth)

A beautifully illustrated edition of the most famous romance of the supernatural.

ISBN 1 872226 55 8 £4.95

## The Best of Old Lancashire — Poetry & Verse

Published in 1866 as the very best of contemporary Lancashire writing, this book now offers a wonderful insight into the cream of Lancashire literature in the middle of the last century. Nearly 150 years later, edited and republished, the book now presents a unique opportunity to read again the masters of our past.

ISBN 1 872226 50 7 £4.95

## THE STORIES
## AND TALES SERIES

### Stories and Tales Of Old Merseyside
(Frank Hird, edited Cliff Hayes)

Over 50 stories of Liverpool's characters and incidents PLUS a
booklet from 1890 telling of the city's history, well illustrated.
ISBN 1 872226 20 5                               £4.95

### Stories & Tales Of Old Lancashire
(Frank Hird)

Over 70 fascinating tales told in a wonderful light-hearted fashion.
Witches, seiges and superstitions, battles and characters all here.
ISBN 1 872226 21 3                               £4.95

### Stories and Tales Of Old Manchester
(Frank Hird, edited Cliff Hayes)

A ramble through Manchester's history, many lesser known stories
brought to life, informative yet human book. Over 50 stories.
ISBN 1 872226 22 1                               £4.95

### Stories Of Great Lancastrians
(written Frank Hird)

The lives of 24 great men of the county, told in easy reading style.
Complete with sketches and drawings, a good introduction to the
famous of Lancashire and Manchester. John Byrom, Arkwright, Tim
Bobbins, Duke of Bridgewater.
ISBN 1 872226 23 X                               £4.95

### More Stories Of Old Lancashire
(Frank Hird)

We present another 80 stories in the same easy, readable style, very
enjoyable, great. With special section for Preston Guild 1992.
ISBN 1 872226 26 4                               £4.95

# LANCASHIRE 150
# YEARS AGO

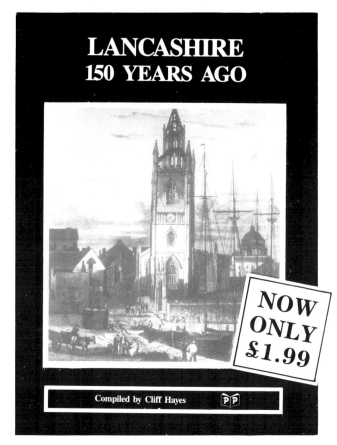

A great addition to the collection
of any lover of Lancashire's
history

# The History of Lancashire Cookery

## by Master Chef Tom Bridge

## Printwise Publications Limited

*Well known Master Chef Tom Bridge turns his attention to his home county. As each recipe takes us deep into Lancashire's culinary past he reveals the history and the tales which surround the classic dishes of the region.*

This book is dedicated to Her Royal Highness the Princess Anne. A donation will be made from the royalties of this book to the Save the Children Fund, Princess Anne's favourite charity.

*Includes a facsimile reprint of the U.C.P. Tripe Recipe Book from 1934.*

# SONGS OF
## A Lancashire Warbler
by
Lowell Dobbs

Hoo seet mi heart gooin' back an' forrit,
 Thumpin' like a facthry mule-
Then hoo spun her charms areawnd it
 Like silk areawnd a spool.

£4.95

*look out for...*

*Also coming shortly...*

## "*Getting to Know*
## THE LAKE DISTRICT"